Accelerated Learning:
Proven Scientific Techniques to Learn Absolutely Anything.

Unlock Your Hidden Potential For Unlimited Memory

Kevin Powell

CONTENTS

INTRODUCTION

This book is about learning how to learn. Whether you want to improve your grades at school, or you want to pick up a new subject quickly, this book will detail methods to learn any kind of subject matter lighting fast. Today, it is commonly said that in order to master a subject, you must dedicate a minimum of 10,000 hours, whether it's to learn a musical instrument, a sport or to master a video game. But there are methods that reduce the time it takes to master a subject, or at the very least become proficient. I am not saying you'll learn to master a subject within the space of a week, that would be impossible. But I am saying you can learn what would usually take months, in weeks.

You may think it's difficult to achieve 100% in a test. Actually it's not as difficult as you think, I have done it myself multiple times throughout secondary school, (the UK equivalent to high-school). You don't need to be particularly intelligent to be a high achieving student. Why? Because most high school tests are about regurgitating information from memory, as sad as that is, it means that if you have the capacity to store large quantities of information with your brain, there is nothing stopping you from achieving that 100%.

You may be thinking, your too old to improve your learning. The answer to that is no, there is no age limit when it comes to improving your learning capabilities. Anyone, no matter the age can benefit greatly from improving their memory. The ability the absorb and process information may seem like a simple thing, but it is what has allowed mankind to become the most dominant species on the planet. The human brain holds immense potential, and this book is designed to unlock that hidden potential, which in turn will allow you to learn ridiculously fast. So fast you will be amazed you had it within you.

Learning is not purely about memorizing information, if it was then machines would have taken our jobs a long time ago. Learning is also about creating, exploring and looking at things from different perspectives. In this book you will learn the following:

- How to set up the perfect learning environment and why a good learning environment is key to fast learning.

- How your brain learns, and how you can accelerate the learning process.

- What is means to be a learner

- What is memory and how you can expand your memory in ways you've never thought before.

- How to keep on learning throughout the rest of your life

- What we can learn from the greatest thinkers of our time.

BECOMING A LEARNER

What does it take to become a learner? You may think that you stop learning after finishing compulsory education, a lot of people do. But that attitude is what leads people to work unsatisfying jobs, just so they can get by in life without exploring all that the world has to offer. This is not a good attitude to have. Life has a lot more to offer than anyone can ever know and you should make it your goal to learn as much as you can with the time you have on Earth. Albert Einstein once said "Once you stop learning, you start dying".

Learning has never been easier. You have access to the collective knowledge of all of humanity in your front pocket. The internet has revolutionized the way we learn. Next time you get stuck with a question and want to find the answer, consult the internet. I am 99% certain that somebody else has asked the exact same question as you and someone has gave an answer. If you can't find the answer to your question on the internet? Then ask someone, whether it's a real life expert or an online one, they will answer your question because that is what people enjoy doing . The ability and desire to share information and do so willingly is what separates man from beast.

You can learn in a multitude of ways, in todays day and age there are more ways to learn than ever. But there is one way of learning that trumps all others, and that's by learning from exploration. When you explore something, it means that you enjoy it, otherwise you would never bother exploring it in the first place. What if you're unable to explore? Maybe you enjoy being at home or you're not in a position to go out and explore the world. That's fine, as there are many other ways to explore the world. For example, reading a book. Whether it's fiction or non-fiction you're exploring are world you enjoy and you're learning from it.

There are many benefits when it comes to becoming a constant learner, one of them is that you will never become bored, or you will least find it extremely difficult to become bored, because whenever you do get bored you will find something to learn.

You will be a happier person. Learning is not easy, it can be difficult and you may want to give up. But nothing feels better than the sense of accomplishment you get for reaching your goals. The feeling you get from writing a piece of software and it comes out bug free or winning a difficult game of tennis is indescribable. Good things come with time, and mastering a subject will teach you that. Studies have shown that the more ambitious we are, the happier we are. This can be attributes to the fact that ambitious people always have a goal to look forward to, meaning no matter what situation they're in, they see a light at the end of the tunnel. You will be way more humble. When your goal in life is to learn, you will be much more appreciative of everything around your, because you know what it takes. The next time you talk to someone, try to learn from them as they're trying to learn from you. Think of every social interaction as a learning experience no matter their background, education or experience. Because there is always something they know that you don't. And your goal should be to extract that knowledge and take it for yourself. I'm not telling to go around interrogating people for information. But ask questions, and be observant. In addition to becoming humble, you will be a much more likeable person and that will show in your conversations with people. Instead of talking about yourself, talk about them, and their interests. The fact that you're so interested in them will make you seem like a genuine and likable person.

You become an amazing teacher. One of the best things you can do in life is to pass down your knowledge to others, in a way you become immortalized. Because in turn, the person you just taught may go in to teach others and the chain continues. Teaching does not only benefit the student, it benefits the teacher too, as more often than not you will be asked question you've never thought of before and find you're learning something new in the search of the answers to the question. You become a valuable member of society. The fact that you're willing to learn, and enjoy doing so means you hold something of value to everyone, and as you get older that value only increases. You'll find it easier to get a high paying job, because you're willing to learn. You'll find it easier to find a lovely spouse, because you're willing to learn. If you're willing to learn everything will become easier. Which is why it's so important to never stop learning.

VISUAL AUDITORY AND KINESTHETIC

If we're going by dictionary definition, learning is the acquisition of knowledge or skills through study, experience or being taught. But learning goes much beyond this definition as different people learn in different ways. When it comes to preferred learning methods, people can be put into three different categories, visual, auditory and kinesthetic. This is know as the VAK theory of learning. It is important to note that these categories categorize peoples preferred method of learning, so even if you're a visual learner, you can still learn using an auditory approach.

According to VAK theorist, people have a dominant way of learning which falls under one or two of the VAK categories. But the learners preferred way of learning can change depending on the subject they're trying to learn. For example when it comes to sport, someone may prefer the kinesthetic approach, meaning they prefer physically taking part in the activity. But the same person may also prefer the visual approach when it comes to learning how code software.

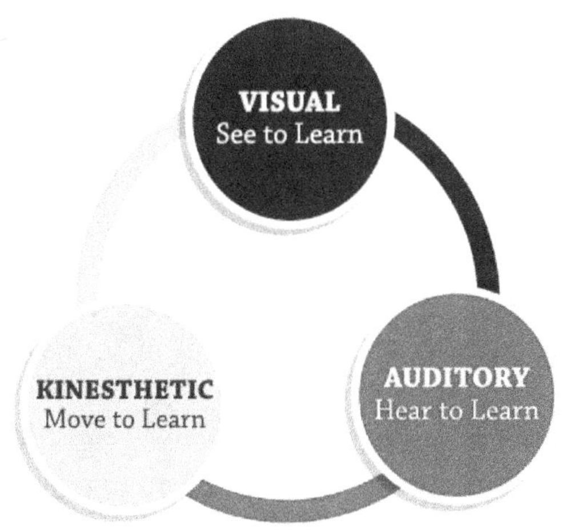

The VAK method of learning is forced upon us throughout school. From kindergarten to third grade you get taught kinesthetically and from fourth grade to eighth grade you get taught visually. After that you get taught auditorily through lectures. Usually you know what your dominant style of learning is by the time you're in high school, but if you don't I recommend you find by paying close attention to how you naturally want to learn the next time you're learning.

Auditory learners tend to prefer learning through audio. They may find that they talk to themselves often. When they read they find it hard do it in their head and resort to reading aloud. They prefer listing to audiobooks over reading, even when they're in a position to read. If you're a auditory learner then you should devise techniques that rely heavily on audio. Group activities and discussion allow you to discuss with your team members. Reading aloud may prove to be more useful than reading in your head, so it might be a good idea to find a place where you can read aloud without disturbing others around you. Try putting new material in a rhythmic pattern, such as a poem or rap. While studying you might find yourself listing to songs. If you do, connect these song with the material you're studying. This means the next time you hear that song, the first thing that comes to mind is the material you was studying while listing to it.

There are two sub-channels when it comes to visual learning, linguistic and spatial. Linguistic visual learners prefer to learn through written language, such as reading and writing. They tend to remember what was written down, even after only reading through it once. Spatial visual learners on the other hand have difficulty with written language and prefer their learning material in the form of graphs, videos and demonstrations. They tend to be very artistic and may find themselves doodling on the page when they're bored. If you're a visual learner you will benefit from using pictures and illustrating your notes in the form of graphs and diagrams. Visual learners find themselves getting easily distracted, so it is a good idea to avoid sitting close to windows when learning and turning off your phone and any other device your find yourself being distracted with. When you're taking notes of the subject material, it's important you emphasis key points by either using a highlighter or underlining. You may find yourself bored while sitting in a lecture and listing to the monotonous voice of the lecturer, even if you find the subject interesting you feeling like falling asleep. If this happens, and you're not retaining any information, it is a good idea to research the subject in your own time using mediums you enjoy. This may be in the form of a YouTube video, podcast or book.

Just like how there are two sub-channels for visual learning, there are also two sub-channels kinesthetic learning, there's your ordinary kinesthetic learners that prefer learning by movement and performing physical activities. Then there is tactile kinesthetic learners that learn by touch. A kinesthetic learner may find themselves losing concentration when there's little to no movement or stimulation. When reading on a subject they may find themselves quickly scanning over the page to find so they can get an idea of the subject matter, instead of taking the time to find the details. When taking notes they often use colored highlighter pens and just like visual learners they may find themselves doodling a lot. If you're a kinesthetic learner it's important to avoid getting bored by taking frequent breaks. Do some physical activity in between studying to physically stimulate your body. You may find that having a fidget toy such as squishy ball can help you stay focused and concentrated.

THE PERFECT LEARNING ENVIROMENT

A good learning environment is not something to be underestimated because it is what allows you to make the most out of your opportunity to learn. A learning environment is somewhere you feel safe and undistracted, such a place could be your classroom, home or study area. You may be thinking, "how am I supposed to create a good learning environment in the classroom? Isn't that the teachers job?" Well, the environment also includes the people within it, so yes, you can help make a better learning environment as a student. There are 9 characteristic all good learning environments share, the first being to always ask questions, no matter how silly it may sound. Being able to ask question is crucial to make the most out of a learning session, it shows you have natural curiosity and with that, a desire to learn. Many people tend to avoid asking questions, because they don't want to seem uneducated or they think there question is too dumb to be worth an answer, but this could not be further from the truth. Brilliant thinkers never stop asking questions, because they know it is the single, most effect way of learning. Many of the worlds greatest thinkers asked nothing but questions. Albert Einstein posed the question, "What would the universe look like if I rode through it on a beam of light?". This lead to the theory of relativity. Isaac Newton posed the question, "Why does an apple fall from a tree?", this lead to the law of gravity. Charles Darwin posed the question, "Why do the Galapagos islands have so many species not found elsewhere?", this lead to the theory of evolution.

Value Questions over answers. As previously mentioned, there is no such thing as a bad question and sometimes, the question may not immediately have an answer. The answer may come days, weeks, month after the question is asked, heck, the question might not even have an answer. But the mere act of questioning brings value, because you're exploring the subject, and there's a slight chance you may bring up a question that's never been thought of before. And when that happens, the subject just gets more interesting. Remember discoveries are founded upon questions, not answers.

Think divergently. Divergent thinking allows for the creation of different ideas about a topic. In order to think divergently, one must be prepared to break down the topic into small, manageable components so each aspect of the topic can be analyzed on it's own. A technique used to generate ideas from divergent sources are brainstorms, a technique that involves generating a list of ideas from multiple sources in an unstructured manner. No idea should be rejected in a brainstorm, because even though the idea may not seem plausible, it may branch off into new ideas that are plausible.

Use a wide variety of learning models. Sometimes you'll want to switch up the way you learn, this can be done by using a wide variety of learning models. For example, when learning about a new programming language, you want to avoid learning just through just a textbook, for one thing the textbook may be outdated. You'll want to switch it up by doing some online research on the language, asking a peer and learning from them, doing some experimentation by coding yourself. Using a wide variety of learning models avoid you from getting burned out and can keep the subject interesting and engaging.

Think real world scenarios. When you're learning, it's important to try and connect the learning material to the real world. Learning about a fiction novel? Try connecting the characters to people you know, good stories always have believable characters that fall under an architype, sometimes these fictional characters can be connect to real life people and can help you learn more about them.

Personalize your learning to fit the criteria. You want to develop a learning method that makes the most sense for the material you're learning. If you're learning about a sport, you'd want to prioritize practice and physical learning over theoretical learning. If you're learning about a science such as chemistry you'd want to as much visual or auditory learning as possible, but also throw in their a couple practical lessons. Tailor your leaning method to you subject.

Be persistent in your assessment. After every learning session, think to yourself what have I learned at what have I still to learn? Admit when you have struggled to learn a certain topic, think of the reason for your struggle and how you can overcome it for your next learning session. Test yourself periodically. Find a list of questions you find difficult and try to answer them. Found the questions too hard? Keep on practicing. Found it too easy? Find harder questions. Get feedback from peers or mentor. What they can tell should be treated like gold.

The goal for success should be transparent. You should always have a goal in mind. Whether it is to have the highest grade among your peers, or it's to get your dream job. The path towards your goal should be clear and you should know what it takes to achieve it.

Ensure you have plenty opportunities to practice. The ultimate tool for learning is practice and you should make sure you give yourself as many opportunities as possible to practice. This can be done in a variety of ways. Surround yourself with people who have an interest for the subject you want to learn. You will find that their knowledge of the subject will naturally brush of on you. What better way to learn how to fish than to surround yourself with fisherman. You also want to give yourself time to practice. Get into the habit of scheduling your week so that you have enough time to practice.

Keep your environment tidy. No one want's to learning in a disorganized, chaotic mess. By keeping your environment tidy and organized will help you focus on your studies. A clean room results in a clean mind.

Bringing all these characteristic together will ensure your learning environment is as perfect as possible. Be sure you keep these in mind and you will find you capability to learn increase immensely.

THE BRAIN AND LEARNING

Learning how your brain learns can be extremely useful when it comes to finding out your preferred method of learning. This chapter will cover things you should know about your brain when it comes to learning.

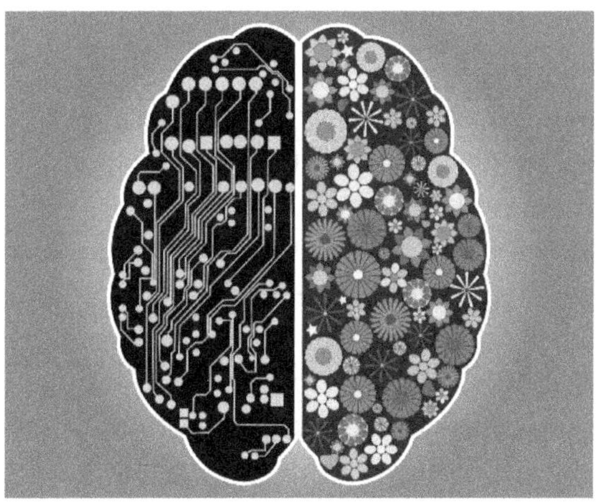

First, we will cover some of the basics of the brain. The brain contains approximately 86 billion nerve cells, also known as neurons. A nerve cell receives information from other nerve cells or sensory organs and sends information to other nerve cells. The largest part of the human brain is the cerebrum, which makes up for 85 percent of the brain's weight. The cerebrum is divided into two hemispheres, which are connected to each other by the corpus collosum. Strangely enough, the left hemisphere controls the right side of the body and the right hemisphere control the left side of the body. The left hemisphere of the brain is said to handle logical tasks such as reading, writing, speaking and arithmetic understanding. Where as the right side of the brain is said to handle more creative tasks, such as visual perception, pattern recognition, music and emotional expression.

It is said that people can left or right brain dominant, just like they can be left and right hand dominant. A person who is "left brained" is said to be more logical, analytical and objective. A person who is "right brained" is said to be more thoughtful, intuitive and subjective. As it turns out, the theory of left brain and right brain dominance is simply a psychology myth that grew from observations of the human brain that were dramatically distorted. But it's interesting how this myth is still widely popular despite being debunked. Nonetheless, understanding your strengths and weaknesses can help you develop better ways of learning. For example, if you find it difficult to listen to a lecture, it might be useful to write down what is being said and reviewing your notes.

So how does your brain learn? To answer that question one must be familiar with plasticity, to be more specific, neuroplasticity. Neuroplasticity is the brains ability to change and grow throughout life. Whenever you learn something new, your brain changes physically by strengthening it's neural connections, as well as creating new connections. Imagine you're learning how to play the guitar for the first time ever. Your brain has its work cut out for it. It has to process all of your senses – what you feel, hear and see. You will be thinking about all things to need to be thinking about to play the guitar. Your motor skills will be put to the test trying to string the guitar. You will be listening to your music, and how the sounds coincide with your figure movements. Your brain will be storing precise timings and co-ordinates the movements need. Your brain will be developing new neural connections in order to better memorize the musical actions. All these things are going on simultaneously in your brain without you even realizing it. The first couple times you pick up the guitar, you're bound to make some mistakes. But with practice, your brain will develop and strengthen neural connections devoted to playing the guitar. The more your practice the stronger the neural connection becomes, until you finally master the art of playing the guitar. This is how learning is done.

There are some things you should know about the brain to make the most out of your learning sessions which will help speed up the neural strengthening of your brain. Humans are visual creatures, out of all of our senses we rely on vision the most. So it makes sense that humans process visual information the best. This is because the brain has A LOT of neurons devoted to visual processing. Around 30 percent of the neurons in the cortex are devoted solely on processing visual information. That's a large chunk of your brain devoted to processing the information from your eyes. Humans are also very sensitive to movement, we've evolved that way to avoid being ambushed by predators. Today we don't have to worry about being preyed upon by ambush predators, but we still have a keen sense for movement. So it may come as no surprise that videos and visualizations are a great way to learn.

We tend to forget little details. When you're learning something new, it is easy to get too caught up in the details and get overwhelmed. A way to avoid this is to look at the big picture. When you're learning new information, the brain may forget things if it can't find prior knowledge to something relatable. So when you look at the big picture, it gives your brain something to go back and relate to when processing new information. There's a metaphor that may help you visualize this concept. Imagine your brain is like a closet of shelves, as you add more clothes they fill up more of the shelf and you start to categorize them. If you add new information, such as a black sweater, it can go on the black shelf, winter shelf or sweater shelf. In real life you cant put the clothes on more than one shelf but in your brain that new piece of information gets linked to existing concepts and you're more easily able to remember the new piece of information.

Sleeping affects learning capability. Studies have shown that getting a good night's sleep in between learning sessions can significantly increase your brains ability to retain information. In a study on motor skills, it was found that participants that got a good night's sleep 12 hours after learning something new improved their abilities by 20 percent. The participants that were tested at 4 hour intervals during the day were found to only increase their abilities by 4%. So the next time you're studying or have a test, make sure you're well rested. Finding it difficult to get a good nights sleep? Try to take naps during the day. Studies have shown that taking naps have the same benefits as getting a full nights sleep. Sleep before a learning session also had great benefits. Dr. Matthew Walker, a lead researcher from the University of California has said "Sleep prepares the brain like a dry sponge, ready to soak up new information". If there's one thing you want to avoid when learning a new skill, it's sleep deprivation. Studies have shown that sleep deprivation has a huge negative impact when it comes to learning a new skill as it cuts the learning capabilities of the brain by as much as 40 percent. So before learning a new skill, make sure you get some good rest and if you can't, make sure to make up for it by taking naps. This is so you can make the most of your learning session.

The brain learns best when teaching others. When you're teaching others, you tend to organize information a little differently in your mind and recalling information becomes easier. In one study done by Dr. John Nestojko, half the participants were told they would be tested on a subject they were learning. The other half were told they have to teach someone else what they have learned. Both sets of participates actually had to do a test so they didn't actually have to teach anyone. Interestingly, it was found that the group of participants that were told they had to teach someone scored higher marks than the group that were told they were being tested. This implies that the mindse of the learner before learning can make a big impact on the learners learning capabilities. So the next time you're learning, try fooling yourself into thinking you're going to have to teach to other people, or better yet actually teach other people. That way not only are you benefitting yourself with an increased learning capability, but you're also benefitting somebody else my teaching them.

WHAT IS MEMORY?

What exactly is memory? It's a tough question to answer, but put simply, memory is a process that involves storing, acquiring and recalling information. Not all memory is the same however. There are actually three types of memory. Sensory, short term and long term. But before we dive into the different types of memory lets look a little deeper into what memory actually is.

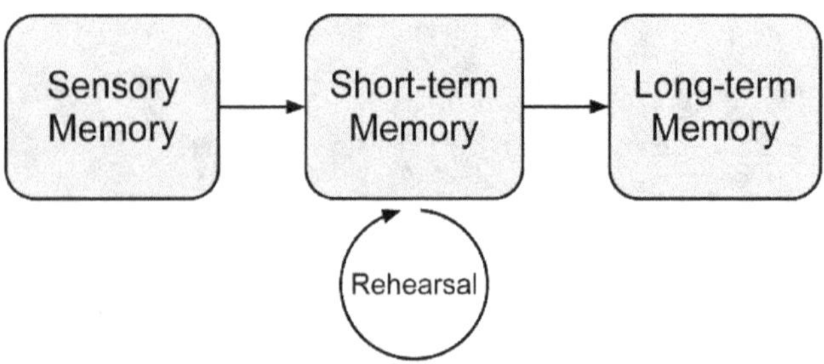

We can break down the process of memory into three parts, encoding, storage and retrieval. When information goes from a sensory input to our brain, it needs to change form so that the brain can understand, process and store it. Think of it like exchanging currency when you're travelling to a different country. The currency of your home country is useless unless you have it converted. There are three ways this information can be encoded which are visually, acoustically and semantically. How do you remember a telephone number? If you see the number, then that means you're using visual encoding, but if you're repeating it to yourself verbally you're using acoustic encoding. Evidence suggests that the primary encoding method for short term memory is acoustic. This means when a person is rehearsing for something, like a play or concert, the information is held in short term memory and they'll forget it soon after the play or concert. The primary encoding method for long term memory is semantic, which is when you give something meaning. This means that giving meaning to information helps you retain that piece of information for far longer.

How long does memory last for? According to research, most adults can store 5 to 9 items in their short term memory. People used to think that memory kind of worked like slots, and that the maximum number of slots for short term memory was 7. But, if we connect pieces of information together, we can hold a lot more information in short term memory. Unlike short terms memory, long term memory is thought to be pretty much limitless.

How is memory retrieved? Everyone has forgotten something, whether it's forgetting to bring your calculator to a math test, or forgetting your keys in the car. The brain forgets almost every day. Forgetting is when the brain fails to retrieve information. The way your brain retrieves from short term memory and long term memory are very different. Short term memory is retrieved sequentially. This means when somebody is asked to remember a list of numbers, and then is asked to remember the 6th number in the sequence, they will go through all numbers in the order they heard to get to the 6th number. By contrast, long term memory is stored by association. This means if you go upstairs, and suddenly forgot why you went upstairs, going back into the room where you first though about going upstairs can jog your memory and make you remember why you wanted to go upstairs. Keeping information organized can help when it comes to retrieving information from the brain. Organizing means keeping records of time, sorting alphabetically or by size. If somebody has given you a list of tasks to do, sorting them out in a sequence, such as a sequence of time can make it easier to memorize. A lot of people think they know about memory. But the truth of the matter is that memory is very strange and scientist are just now starting to understand it. This means a variety of myths have been spread among the people and you need to know how to tell apart myth from fact.

Myth number one. Memory is like a video recorder.

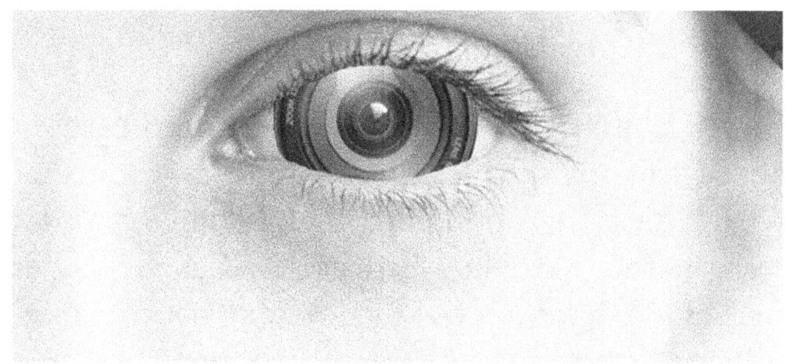

Many people fall under the assumption that memory behaves like a video recorder, and the eye is the lens. This is a common misconception among people, after all a video recorder is the closest thing relatable to memory for a lot of people. In a US survey more than 63 percent of participates said they strongly believe that memory works like a video camera in the sense that it accurately records everything we see and hear. This cannot be further from the truth. Memory is in fact a very fickle thing as it can be easily distorted and manipulated. Researchers Bernstein and Loftus examined half a dozen studies that examined whether researchers could plant false memories into people. The false memories in question were to do with food preferences, such as liking asparagus despite never trying it. In one experiment, the participants completed questionnaires that included a personality and food history test. A week later they were brought back to the lab and told their answers were fed into a machine that generated a profile of their childhood experiences with food. One of the findings were that they either got sick after eating hard-boiled eggs or they felt ill after eating dill pickle. After learning about this, the participants completed the same food history questionnaire. The participants that were falsely told they had gotten sick from dill pickles or hard-boiled egg showed significantly less preference towards those food items.

Myth number 2, people can have photographic memory. It's a common belief that some people have a natural talent to take photographs with their brain and are then able to retrieve the photos with 100 percent accuracy. This is of course not the case. There are some amazing feats of memorization, such as memory champion Lu Chao who set the world record for reciting pi to the 67,890[th] digit. But unfortunately, Lu Chao does not posses photographic memory. What has allowed Lu Chao to achieve such incredible feats can be put down to the use of mnemonic devices and thousands upon thousands of hours practicing.

Myth number 3, people forget things over time.

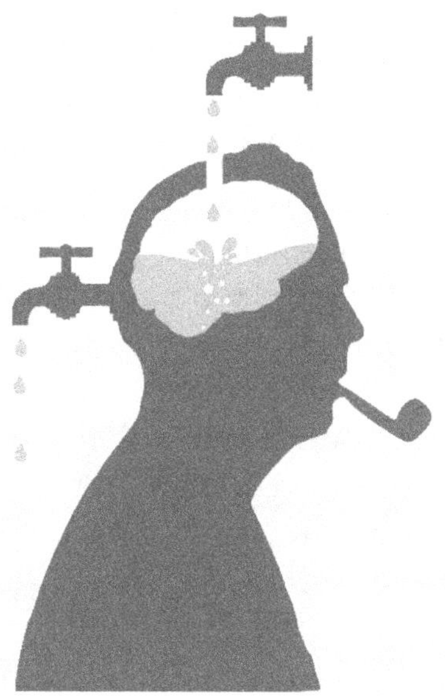

Many people think memories decay over time. Studies reveal that memories do not degrade like a reel of film. Most memories are forgotten almost instantly after an event. For this reason, eye witness testimonies are not held to a high regard in the court of law.

Myth number 4, confidence indicates an accurate memory. Being confident that your recollection is accurate does not mean it is. There are factors that can increase you confidence in a memory despite it not being accurate, such as repeated questioning. Being asked the same question over and over again and giving the same answer again and again has the side effect of making you believe what you're saying is right. Everyone has different levels of confidence when it comes to memory recollection. Somebody can be very confident in their memory, despite being wrong most of the time. Likewise, someone can have very low confidence is their memory even though they're right. Another related myth is that having an emotional experience leads to more accurate memories. Memories connected to an emotional experience often are remembered more vividly, making people confident that things went exactly how they remembered them. But in actuality, these memories are just as prone to being distorted as any other.

Myth number 5, traumatizing memories are repressed and can be recovered years after they have occurred. Many people believe that traumatic experiences, such as an abusive childhood are repressed deep within the brain and can be somehow recovered with the help of a hypnotist. Studies on child abuse victims suggest they, in fact do not forget traumatic experience. When somebody has a memory "recovered" it is far more likely that the memory in question has been fabricated or highly distorted. Memories cannot be recovered by a hypnotist for the same reason why memory does not behave like a video recorder. We do not remember every detail. In fact, evidence has suggest that hypnotism can do more harm than good by giving people a confidence boost in their memory, whether the memory is accurate or not.

Myth number 6, Amnesiacs forget who they are. The idea that people who suffer from amnesia lost their long term memory is a myth that's been dramatized by Hollywood. The fact is, amnesiacs do not possess the ability to create new memories. To be more specific, they lack the ability to convert short term memories into long term memories. This is why an amnesiac may be able to tell you about their early lives but they have trouble when it comes to remembering what they ate for lunch.

IMPROVING MEMORY

In this chapter, I will go over ways you can increase your memory capacity. It's important to remember that some method may work better for you than others, so it's a good idea to try them all until you've found ones that work for you. But first I will go over some small tips to help boost your brain power.

Give your brain a good workout.

Just like muscles, your brain will deteriorate if you don't use it consistently, which is why it's important you give your brain daily stimulation. The best brain exercises are the ones that break your usual routine and force you out of your comfort zone, as these exercises will create new neural pathways, strengthening your brain. A good brain exercise will teach your something new. If you exercise your brain by doing something you're already good at, you're not exercising much at all. The brain exercise needs to be challenging, and you should have to give it your full attention. The exercise should not be something you can do without giving it your full mental effort. It would be good if it's a skill you can improve upon. Look for brain activities that allow you to start at a low level and slowly work your way up. Always try to push your metal capabilities to the limit. When an activity is starting to get too easy, move on to the next level. Make sure the brain activity is rewarding. Rewarding yourself is a great way to learn. The more interested you are in an activity, the more you will engage and try to improve yourself. So it's a good idea to choose an activity you find enjoyable and you want to improve yourself with. A good brain workout does not have to be something intense like chess, although that is a totally viable option. Learning how to play the guitar, dance or speak Spanish are also viable options when it comes to giving your brain a good workout. The most important thing is that it's something that stimulates your brain and you enjoy doing it.

You brain is not the only thing that needs to be exercised, your body needs it too. Studies have shown that physical exercise is extremely important for brain health. It increases the amount of oxygen available to your brain and reduces the risk of illnesses that result in memory loss such as diabetes. The reason why you should exercise if you want to keep your brain in tip top condition has to do with neuroplasticity. Exercising regularly has shown to play an important role in the development and growth of neural connections. Choose physical activities that get your heart pumping such as aerobic exercises. Exercising after waking up is a great way to start the morning and helps prepare your brain for learning throughout the day. Next time you take a break from studying, try going out for a short walk or do a couple jumping jack. You will find that doing a small amount of exercise in between break can help reduce mental fatigue so when you get back from your break you'll feel refreshed and ready to learn.

Get enough sleep. Adults need at least 7.5 hours of sleep to avoid becoming sleep deprived. Losing even a few hours of sleep can negatively affect your brains performance. When you become sleep deprived, your ability to think, remember, problem solve and be creative are reduced significantly. Sleep is extremely important when it comes to learning and memory. Studies have shown that sleep is necessary for brain growth and the strengthening of neural connections. During the deepest stage of sleep, your brain activity levels peak as this is the stage where most new neural connections are made. Get into a sleep schedule and stick to it. Go to bed at the same time and wake up at the same time each morning, even when it's the weekend. You will find that by doing this, you will feel much less lethargic in the morning and you'll fall asleep much faster than you're used to. Avoid looking at screens before going to bed. I know this may seem difficult for a lot of people, as going on your phone before bed has become a bad habit for a lot of people. But studies have show that blue light emitted from phones, tv's and computer monitors triggers chemicals that inhibit melatonin, a hormone produced by the pineal gland that regulates sleep and wakefulness. Finding it too difficult to give up your phone before sleeping? A lot of phone today include a feature that reduces the amount of blue light emitted by the screen. Although it is preferable you don't use your phone at all before sleeping, if you insist on using your phone make sure you enable this feature. Do you consume a lot of caffeine? You might want to cut back on that if you're having troubles sleeping. Some people have a strong tolerance for caffeine and are able to sleep just fine, but this is a very small percent of the population. If you think caffeine is effecting your sleep, try cutting back and see if it helps.

Socialize and hang out with friends.

Humans are not solitary animals, we thrive on social interaction. Socializing with other people is one of the best exercises you can do for your brain. Studies have shown that having a strong relationship with other people is not only emotionally helpful, but it's also very important for brain health. Research carried out by the Harvard School of Public Health has shown that people who socialize regularly have the slowest rate of memory deterioration. The benefits of social interaction is not exclusive to just human interaction, animal interaction can also help with brain health. Playing with your dog also means your exercising your body, so you hit two birds with one stone!

Stress can wreak absolute havoc on your brains health and can be linked with memory loss. Chronic stress has been shown to destroy brain cells and damage the hippocampus region of the brain, which is the part of the brain used to form and retrieve memories. To avoid stress it's important to set realistic expectations. Don't stress yourself out trying to reach the unreachable, goals are achieved one step at a time. Take breaks often. It's important to realize when you need a break. Many people seem to think taking a break is unproductive, but this is not true. In fact, taking a break can be more productive because it gives you time to refresh your brain, so when you come back from your brake, you're back to working at peak performance. Do not bottle up your feelings. Expressing yourself is a great stress reliever. Harboring bad thoughts inside of you will only make you feel more and more stressed, releasing those thought to someone can lift all that stress off you and you'll feel much better for it. Do not overwork yourself. Set yourself some leisure time so you can do the things you want to do. A good mindset to have is to remember, you work to live not live to work. Focus on one task at a time. Seriously, live in the moment. Focus on doing one thing and doing it well with no distractions, no stress or no burnout. By focusing on a single task your work will become more focused, your productivity will increase and you'll become extremely good at what you do. The idea that multi-tasking leads to more productivity is a myth, it simply gives you the illusion that you're achieving more.

You'll find you'll be much less distracted and are much less likely to procrastinate if you follow the single tasking life. Research has shown that mediation is great for relieving stress. Mediating has been linked to reducing depression, anxiety, diabetes, high blood pressure and can improve focus, memory, concentration and learning ability. The act of meditating has been shown to actually alter the brain. Brain scans from people who meditate on a regular basis have been shown to have more activity in the left prefrontal cortex, which is the region of the brain associated with feelings of happiness. It has also shown that the thickness of the cerebral cortex is on average thicker than non-meditators, resulting in more neural connections and an increased memory and learning capability.

People often say that laughter is the best medicine, well that's true! The act of laughing, engages multiple regions for brain, resulting in more brain activity and a healthier brain.

When you listen to a joke, you're trying to figure out the punchline. This promotes activity in regions of your brain that correspond to learning and creativity. A good way to add more laughter to your life is to start laughing at yourself, don't be afraid to share embarrassing moments in your life. Looking back at times you thought of as stressful and finding the humor in it is a great way to brighten your mood and take yourself less seriously. Spend time with people you enjoy being around. Being around people you connect with and people who make you laugh will make your life a much happier one. People say laughing is contagious, so stick around people who laugh a lot and you're bound to get more laughs in your life.

Eat the foods your brain likes. Brain exercises are not the only thing that can help improve brain memory, a good diet can too. Research has shown that Omega 3 fatty acids can help in improving brain health. Foods that contain omega 3 fatty acids are typically cold water fish such as tuna, salmon, sardines, herring, mackerel and trout. Even you're not a fan of fish, omega 3 fatty acids can also be found in walnuts, seaweed, flaxseed oil, broccoli, spinach, pumpkin seeds and soybeans. Eating more fruits and vegetables can also improve brain health. Fruits are full of anti-oxidants that protect your brain cells from damage. As you age, it gets more difficult for your brain cells to protect themselves against highly reactive components known as free radicals. Every cell in your body creates unstable oxygen molecules, you're also exposed to them through the environment through air pollution. Left unchecked, these free radicals damage cells by a process known as oxidative stress, which is said to be the leading cause of age related metal illnesses. You body combats these free radicals by producing it's own anti-oxidants.

So help your body out by eating more fruits with high amounts of anti-oxidants. Another great way to get more anti-oxidants in your system is to drink green tea. Green tea contains polyphenols, a powerful anti-oxidant, not only do polyphenols protect brain cells from free radicals, they have also been show to help in fighting cancer and reducing inflammation. It may sound weird, but alcohol has been shown to help improve memory and cognition, but too much alcohol has been shown to kill brain cells, speeding up the deterioration of the brain. So stick to wine or grape juice in moderation. Red wine appears to be better than white wine as it is rich in resveratrol, a flavonoid that boosts blood flow.

Health is a big issue when it comes to living a happy lifestyle, there are many diseases that can deteriorate your memory. So it's important to identify any health problem you may think you have as soon as possible so you can reduce it's affects. High blood pressure and cholesterol has been linked to reducing cognitive ability. If you're diagnosed with either of these illnesses be sure to consult your doctor. Many over the counter medications have also been shown to prevent clear thinking and reduced memory recollection. Such medications include, cold and allergy medication as well as anti-depressants. Now I'm not saying to stop taking these medications, but it's good to be aware of there effects on your brain.

ACCELERATED LEARNING

Accelerated learning is just what is sounds like. A way to accelerate your learning using clever techniques that help you easily remember and recall information from your brain.

Chunking is a learning technique that can be defined as chopping down the number of items that need to be remembered. According to research, the average person can hold anywhere between five and nine items in there working memory for up to 20 minutes. Chunking helps solve this issue by reduce the amount of items that needs to be remember. Chunking can be separated into two parts, categorical chunking and pattern chunking. Pattern chunking is when you identify a pattern or order and you use that to help you remember the item. An example of categorical chunking is when learning about mitosis in biology. The five phases of mitosis are interphase, prophase, metaphase, anaphase and telophase. All these words have a pattern, they all end with phase. So by remembering the work phase, you only need to remember the words that come before "phase", reducing the amount of items you need to remember. You may not have realized it but you have been learning using the chunking technique ever since 3rd grade. You might remember being taught how to spell words that end the same way such as might, light and fight. That was learning using pattern chunking!

Categorical chunking is when you group large volumes of information into a small number of categories. This technique can be useful when learning subjects like science or history. When you're learning about the digestive system or the animal cell in biology, you're categorizing them into structures or functions. Governments or biological systems can be categorized into taxonomies or hierarchies.

Practice Testing has been praised by learning experts as being one of the best way to retain information and the most researched learning technique in existence. It simply works. You don't have to be given a test paper and be in a testing environment to do a practice test. You can test yourself anytime and anywhere by questioning and answering yourself in your head. So the next time you're on a walk or driving, try answering questions in your head. Another great way of practice testing is by using flash cards. Flash cards are cards that have a question on one side and the answer on the other. Always carry a deck of cards and use them whenever you have a moment to spare, you can even use digital flash cards so you always have them with you as long as you have your smartphone. Some benefits of the flash card technique are that you receive immediate feedback on whether you answered the question correctly. Chunking also comes into effect when using flash cards. As the subject gets divided into small parts and put on the cards.

Ready to take flash cards to the next level? In the 1970s, Sebastian Leitner developed a method of using flash cards that greatly enhances there effectiveness. In this method, you put your cards into three to five stacks (or boxes). At the start, all your cards are in stack one. When you pick up a card and answer it correctly, you move it to stack two. If you get the answer wrong, study the card and place it at the bottom of stack one. Once you've correctly answered all the cards in stack one, move onto stack two. If you can an answer right move the card to stack three. If you get it wrong the card gets demoted and goes back into stack one. Repeat this until you finally get to the last stack. If you get a card wrong in stacks two, three, four or five, they get demoted all the way to stack one. The great thing about Leitner's technique is that it forces you to answer the questions you know the least about more often than the questions you always get right. When you're studying it's always important to focus on your weakest topics and a lot of people forget that. When you've answered all the question and they're all in the highest stack, demote them all back to stack one. Start over again but this time it's all about speed. Time yourself while your answering questions and repeat until it becomes like second nature.

There are two theories about why practice testing works so well. Theory one is testing triggers a complex retrieval process by accessing your long term memory and by doing so, it greatly enhances your ability to retain information. Theory two is that testing promotes the encoding of more effective mediators by the use of targets and cues. There's also evidence to suggest that by practice testing, people are more effectively able to organize information in their brain, making retrieving information a lot more faster and efficient. When you're practice testing, do not keep testing yourself with little time in between tests, studies have shown that practice testing is a lot more effective when you leave an appropriate amount of time in between tests.

Distributed Practice is a learning technique where you divide your studies over a period of time, as opposed to doing all of your studying in one large chunk. Studies have shown that distributed practice is far better than cramming for retaining and absorbing information. There are a few theories as to why this is the case. The study-phase retrieval theory suggests that each time you encounter a piece of information, your brain attempts to retrieve from memory and if the retrieval is successful the memory becomes stronger. When you cram information, the memory is still fresh in you brain so you don't get benefit of retrieving information. Another reason for why distributed practice is better than cramming has to do with contextual variability. When you're learning and your brain is encoding information, the surrounding context is also being encoded. This can serve as a cue later on for retrieving information. When you cram all the information in a day, your surrounding does not change, so the surrounding context remains the same. Perhaps the most convincing reason has to do with the fact that when you're studying the same thing consecutively, you become too familiar with it, thus you're likely to pay less attention.

A Study in 1979 showed that subjects that distributed 6 study sessions with 30 days intervals in-between scored higher on the test when compared to subjects that distributed 6 study sessions with 1 day intervals in-between. The subjects that crammed the study sessions all in one day scored dramatically lower than both the 1 day interval and 30 day interval subjects.

By combining distributed practice with practice testing you're guaranteed to see a massive jump in your learning ability.

Elaborative Interrogation is the act of asking yourself "why?" to get a better understanding of

the subject matter. You ask yourself a question related to the subject for example, say you're learning about organic chemistry you'll ask yourself the question, "why does carbon like to bond with other elements? How does it bond to other elements? What causes it to bond with other elements?" And so on. You can start using elaborative interrogation by making a list of everything you need to learn for a subject. You then go down the list, asking yourself questions about the things you've written down such as why and how they work. You're bound to find the answers by looking on the internet, if you can't you can always ask an expert. As you get deeper and deeper into the subject, start to link together your answers and explain how they work together. A great way to do this is to compare two ideas and see how they differ and how they're similar. Connect the ideas to your own life experiences. Try to find connections through you day to day life to the ideas you're learning about. Doing this means you're also doing distributed practice, which as discussed previously is a very effective method of learning. So why does elaborative interrogation work? Well it has to do with the fact that asking yourself questions forces you to come up with an answer. It also encourages you to think about the relationships between different ideas and how they differ from one another as well as how they're similar.
The idea of elaborative interaction is to keep

building new connections so you can fully understand the ideas of a subject. A great way to do elaborative interrogation is to ask a curious friend if they have any question on the subject you're learning, it would be even better if this friend had very little knowledge on the subject as that may allow you to answer questions that you wouldn't expect.

Self-explanation is kind of similar to elaborative interrogation. It is the practice of thinking out loud. As you're solving a problem, you talk to yourself to force a conscious awareness of the process your mind is going through. Self-explanation is a very popular technique when is comes to solving abstract problems that don't have a clear cut answer. It's sort of similar to showing your working out after solving a math problem. Like elaborative interrogation, you're asking yourself questions to further your understating of the subject. While elaborative interrogation focuses on how well you're learning something, self-explanation focuses on the process of working out the solution to the problem. Some examples of self-explanation questions could be, "What should I do next? What would be an example of this? What do I need to know to solve this problem? How do I acquire that knowledge?". All these questions are examples of what you want to ask yourself with the self-explanation technique. When you're doing self-explanation, it's a good idea to write down your questions on a piece of paper, then to write down the answers. By writing the question then answering them, you're more committed to remembering the information. People who enjoy making conversation will find self-explanation to be an easy technique to learn. Whereas introverted people might find it a difficult technique to grasp. But no matter if you're introverted or extroverted, learning this technique will prove useful in your journey of learning.

The following techniques are considered to have low efficiency, so they're not required to accelerate your learning, but most of them are easy to learn. So if you have the time, these techniques can come in use.

Highlighting material is a very popular method among students because its extremely easy to implement and takes no little to no effort to do. Highlighting can be done by using a highlighter pen or by underlining. The combination of highlighting and other techniques discussed in this book can amplify it's effectiveness. For example, when you're practice testing, highlight parts of the question that matters the most or you could highlight questions you have the most difficulty in understanding. There are multitude of ways can incorporate highlighting during your studies and it takes very little time to learn.

Summarization is quite self-explanatory. It's the
act of summarizing the topic you're learning. The
benefit of summarizing is that it condenses a lot
of information in a small amount of text. This
makes it much easier and quicker to read.
Highlighting can make the summarization process
a lot easier by targeting the main points. Studies
have shown that summarization helps learning
when it comes to things that include a lot of texts
like essays, but it comes in less useful when it
comes to things that don't require large amounts
of texts, like multiple choice questions. It's
important to get a grasp on the main concepts of
the topic you're studying, Combining
summarizing with practice testing will let take out
all of the unnecessary junk testers enjoy putting in
tests and focus on the actual material.

Rereading is one of my least favorite techniques,
studies have shown that, compared to other
learning techniques, rereading does not do much
to accelerate learning. But if you're going to
reread, make sure to leave sometime between
your first and second read. Studies have shown
that learners benefit most from rereading when
there's a four day gap between the first read and
second. So in those four days you can move onto
a different subject, then on the fourth day go
back and reread. This way you're making the
most out of your time by reading new material, as

well as old.

Keyword Mnemonics, can be quite difficult to learn when compared to the other techniques discussed in this list. The idea of this techniques is to connect some form of imagery to associate to words or terms. Studies have show that this greatly enhances retention and recollection of memory and is a great method of learning a new language, terminologies, or definition. The only negative aspect of this technique is that it takes some effort to train yourself to use. But if you take the time to learn this technique, it will prove to be very valuable and worth the effort.

Imagery can also be used remember whole concepts, instead of just keywords, however studies have shown this to be less effective so it's a good idea to just stick with keyword mnemonics. To make the most of this technique, it's important to use images that are memorable so you're less likely to forget.

LEARNING THROUGOUT LIFE

Lifelong learning is a skill that needs to be developed throughout your life. Most people associate learning with formal education. From an early age we're told to get a good education. While formal education is important, it's not the only kind of learning you should be doing. Throughout your life you'll stumble upon many opportunities to expand your knowledge and develop you skills. Lifelong learner enjoy learning not because they're forced to by their peers, but because they want to. There doesn't need to be reason to learn something, the mere act of learning can be a rewarding experience in of itself.

You may want to learn because you want to develop yourself as a person and develop skills that can help enhance your life, whether it's learning to paint or how to fix a car. You may want to learn because you want to develop yourself professionally, whether you want to move up the ladder or change profession. Put in the time it takes to learn and you'll reap the rewards.

In this chapter you will find out how you can keep learning throughout your life and remain a lifelong learner.

Be committed. Learning is not an easy task, and

no matter what steps you take to improve your leaning capability, you still need to put in the time and there's no overcoming that. The reason why professionals are well respected is because they're committed to their profession, there's no short cuts to acquiring skill. Improving yourself takes discipline and focus. At the end of the day you might just feel like kicking back and relaxing, you tell yourself you've earned it. This is not what lifelong learners do. While it's important to relax and unwind every so often, it's important to allocate times in the day where you're committed to learning and improving yourself. Learning does not have to be a slog. You know the saying "Work smarter not harder"? Well that applies to learning too. By using the skills you've acquired by reading this book you've learned how to learn more efficiently.

Get into the habit of scheduling. Humans are ritualistic being, we love rituals and we use them every day. You waking up in the morning and getting ready for work or school is a ritual. We make our own habits because we love doing what's familiar. You can turn your ritualistic habits into a force for good by making good use of schedules. When you take the time to schedule something you build up an anticipation for it. You make a habit out of sticking to your schedule and you'll find that you can get a lot more in a day. Scheduling helps you stay on task, stay focused and greatly reduces your chances of getting distracted. It also lets other people know what you're doing so they won't be distracting you. The first step in making a schedule is to identify how much time you have to yourself, the more time you have the better. Once you've established your time slots, schedule out the essential actions you need to take. These are things that you consider important above all else. Once you've established the essentials, its's time to schedule the high priority activities. These are activities you consider of high importance and something you cannot miss. Once you've established both your essential and high priority activities, it's time to start planning out some extra time in case of an emergency. If you live a pretty stable life (which is rare) then you probably won't need to leave a lot of extra time. But if you live an unpredictable life then you should know from personal experience how much time you should set aside. Whether you set learning as a high priority or essential priority task is up to you, just make sure you stick to your schedule.

Avoid stress. Stress has been shown to reduce your brains ability to learn. As stress levels increase, you body releases hormones and neurotransmitters that make you over react to danger, causing fear. Trying to learn while stressed out is an impossible task so don't create an environment where you're constantly stressed.

Take time to enjoy the simple things in life and don't make life more complex than it has to be.

Learn because you find it interesting, not because someone else told you. Don't box yourself into believe that you're only good at doing a few things. More likely than not, you're good at many things but you just haven't discovered them. So take the time to explore the world and if you're given the opportunity to learn a new skill, take it. You might just find your hidden talent.

Lifelong learning is not just a skill, it's a life style that can enhance your life tremendously. It makes you more employable, more interesting, more attractive and above all more happy. It enhances your understanding of the world around you and brings you opportunities. We live in an age of machine intelligence, where all information is available at the tip of your finger. The world is rapidly changing and there's never been a better time than now to become a lifelong learner.

LEARNING FROM THE GREATS

This chapter will discuss how the great scientist and inventors of our time acquired their vast amounts of knowledge and what we can learn from their mistakes and achievement. Some of the techniques listed here are not recommended for all people, as many of them were suited to fit the needs of their inventors. But there's still a great deal to be learned and the techniques can be incorporated into your own learning methods.

Richard Feynman is an noble prize winning physicist known for his work in quantum mechanics, theory of quantum electrodynamics and physics of supercooled liquids. He's also the inventor of a mental model for learning known as The Feynman Technique. The technique is designed to help you learn pretty much anything extremely efficiently. The awesome thing about this technique is that it's very simple, easy to learn and it consists of only four steps.

Step 1. Take a blank piece of paper and write the subject that you want to learn. Then write out what you know of the subject using very simple English. Pretend you're writing to explain to a 7 year old who only has the attention span and enough vocabulary to understand basic concepts. By doing this you're eliminating any waffle and complicated jargon used when people don't understand a topic. People often use overly complicated terminology to fool themselves into thinking they're competent in a subject. In actuality, if you're truly competent then you'll be able to explain the subject to 7 year old which is what you're mimicking when you're carrying out this step. By writing like you're explain to a 7 year old, you force yourself to understand the subject at a deeper level by simplifying complex topics, getting to the very essence of the subject.

Step 2. Once you've written down the explanation, take time review it. Pinpoint areas you had trouble explaining. It's important to identify areas where you have gaps in your knowledge so you can fill them. This step is invaluable because it allows you to discover the limits of your knowledge. Once you've discovered this, the real learning starts. Now it's time to go back to the source material and try learning again until you've filled the gaps in your knowledge and you're able to explain the subject to a 7 year old.

Step 3. Now you've reviewed the subject and written it down in simple term. Reread over your writings and make sure you don't find any overly complicated technical jargon. If you think the explanation would confuse a 7 year old then that's good indication that your understanding of the topic is lacking and you should try to fix that.

Step 4. Once you've completed steps 1 – 3, it's time to take on the real test. Try explaining the subject to someone that has little knowledge of it or better yet, try explaining it to an actual child. This is the ultimate test of your knowledge. If you can pull this off without confusing anyone, then that shows you truly understand the subject. However, if it does confuse them, it's important to not get annoyed at them. The failure lies within you so go back to step 1 and try again.

Albert Einstein discoveries in physics were truly revolutionary, he was a genius in every sense of the word. His way of learning was also very interesting and not what you might of expected. He often skipped classes, not because he didn't understand them, but because he'd rather stay at home to solve difficult problems. Einstein didn't learn physics by attending the classroom, but by obsessively playing around with ideas and equations he'd thought of in his head. It goes to show that learning is done by doing, more so than listening.

Einstein's reason for learning was driven by a never ending curiosity. But how did he know if the theories he'd learn about were correct? He'd try to prove it himself! Einstein needed to know what made things actually work and he was willing to test his theories himself. This curiosity is not unique to Einstein, in fact we've all felt the same curiosity he did ever since we were children. When we're children we're curious about anything and everything. Why is the grass green? What does this taste like? Why is the sky blue? We have to be curious because from a survival stand point we need to learn the most about our environment in is little time as possible. But as we get older we lose this natural curiosity, rather, we get it beaten out of us by formal education. But this doesn't always have to be the case and it clearly wasn't for Einstein.

Einstein's way of learning was through thought experiments. One of his most famous thought experiment was of him imagining riding on a beam of light. He asked himself the question, "What would happen to the light beam if he rode along side it at the same speed?". The logical conclusion was that it would appear as if it's not moving at all. But to Einstein, this seemed impossible according to Maxwell's Electromagnetic Equations. His thought experiments were build upon his vast understanding of physics and mathematics and is what allowed him to pick up on things that other, less intuitive physicist could not.

Charles Darwin was a surprisingly mediocre student, but he had a great passion for geology and biology. He was also very adventurous. In 1831 he signed onto a voyage on the HMS Beagle as a naturalist for a five year expedition to explore South America and the Pacific. It was on this voyage where he made his breakthrough discoveries. It's important to remember that back in the days of Darwin, most people lived there entire lives from just a couple of miles from where they were born. Most people were afraid of the unknown, you can say it's an evolutionary adaptation for survival, but Darwin ventured into the unknown and unravel the mysteries that would change how we thought about biology forever.

Despite Dawkins theory of evolution being one of the most successful theories in the history of science, it did have it's flaws. Some aspects were seriously flawed, such as the idea of blending inheritance. But an obscure scientist named Gregor Mendel discovered the key to the mystery of inheritance and published it soon after Darwin's Origin Of Species. Unfortunately, Darwin never came across his work and the two men's work did not come together until half a century later when scientists discovered what Mendel did years before.

Darwin showed that in order to innovate, you need to explore. Do not be afraid of the unknown, be excited for it. Because like Darwin's venture on the HMS Beagle, we have no way of knowing what we will find. The only thing we know for certainty is that we'll learn nothing if we stay put.

ABOUT THE AUTHOR

Computer Engineer / Entrepreneur / Best Selling
Author. Kevin Powell leads multiple online
businesses from the virtual reality industry to student
stationary. Learning has been a passion of his ever
since he coded his first computer game back in 1995.
Since then he has made it his life goal to learn as
much about the world as he can and teach the ways of
lifelong learning to as many people as possible.